Farmstead                                                    Giannetti

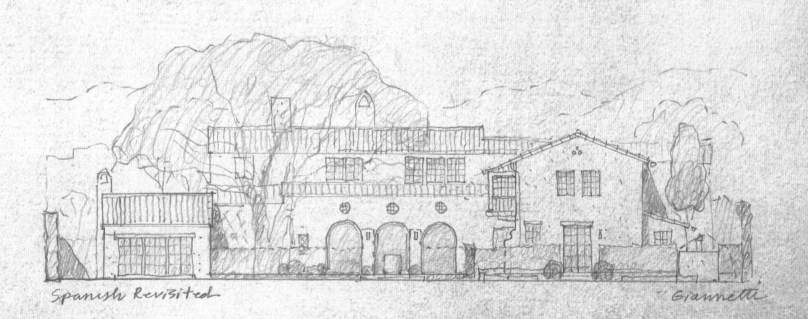

Spanish Revisited                                            Giannetti

*Patina Meadow*                                                        Giannetti

*Tudor Estate*                                                         Giannetti

# Patina
## Homes & Gardens

PHOTOGRAPHY BY
LISA ROMEREIN

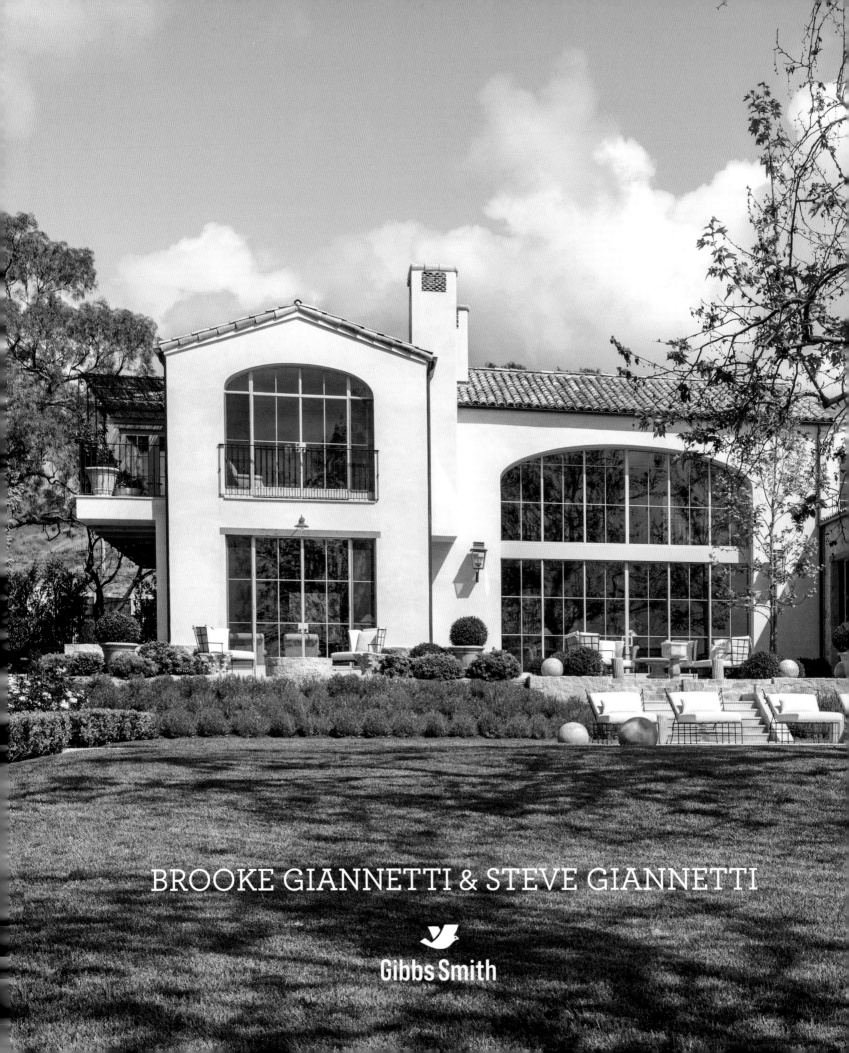

BROOKE GIANNETTI & STEVE GIANNETTI

Gibbs Smith

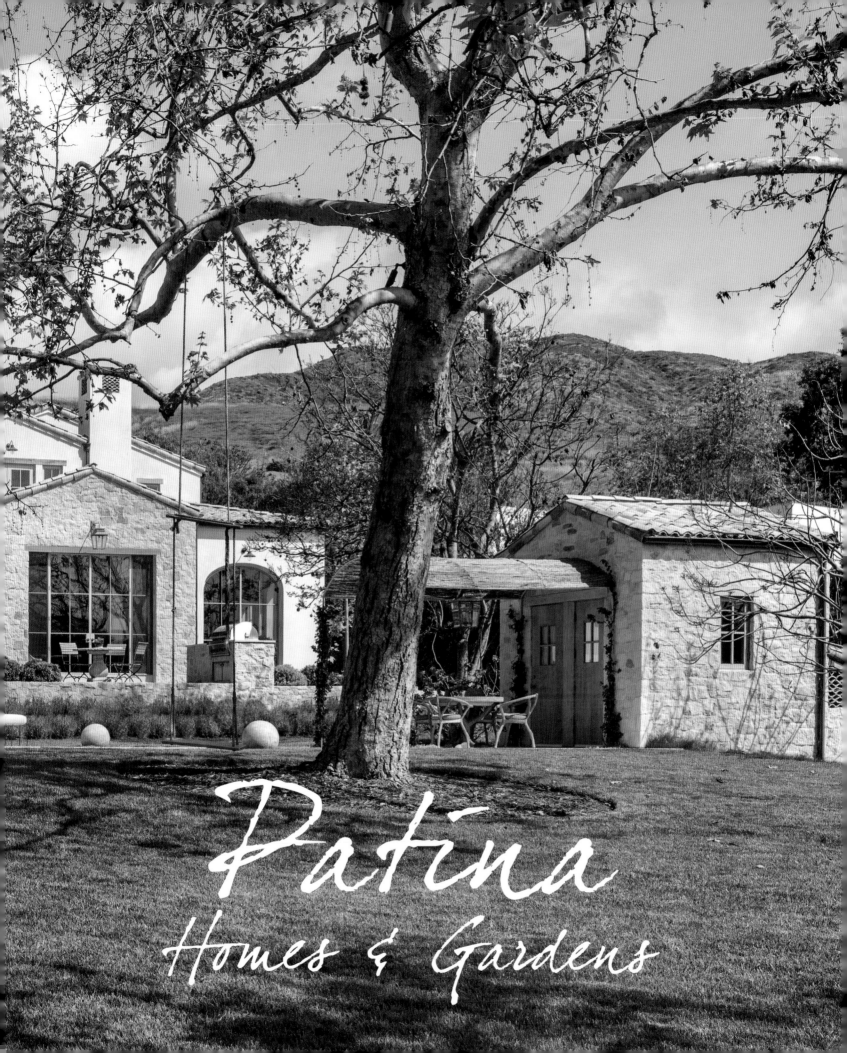

# Patina
## Homes & Gardens

# To all who dream,

including our wonderful

clients, who navigate

through the unknown

to manifest the lives

they envision

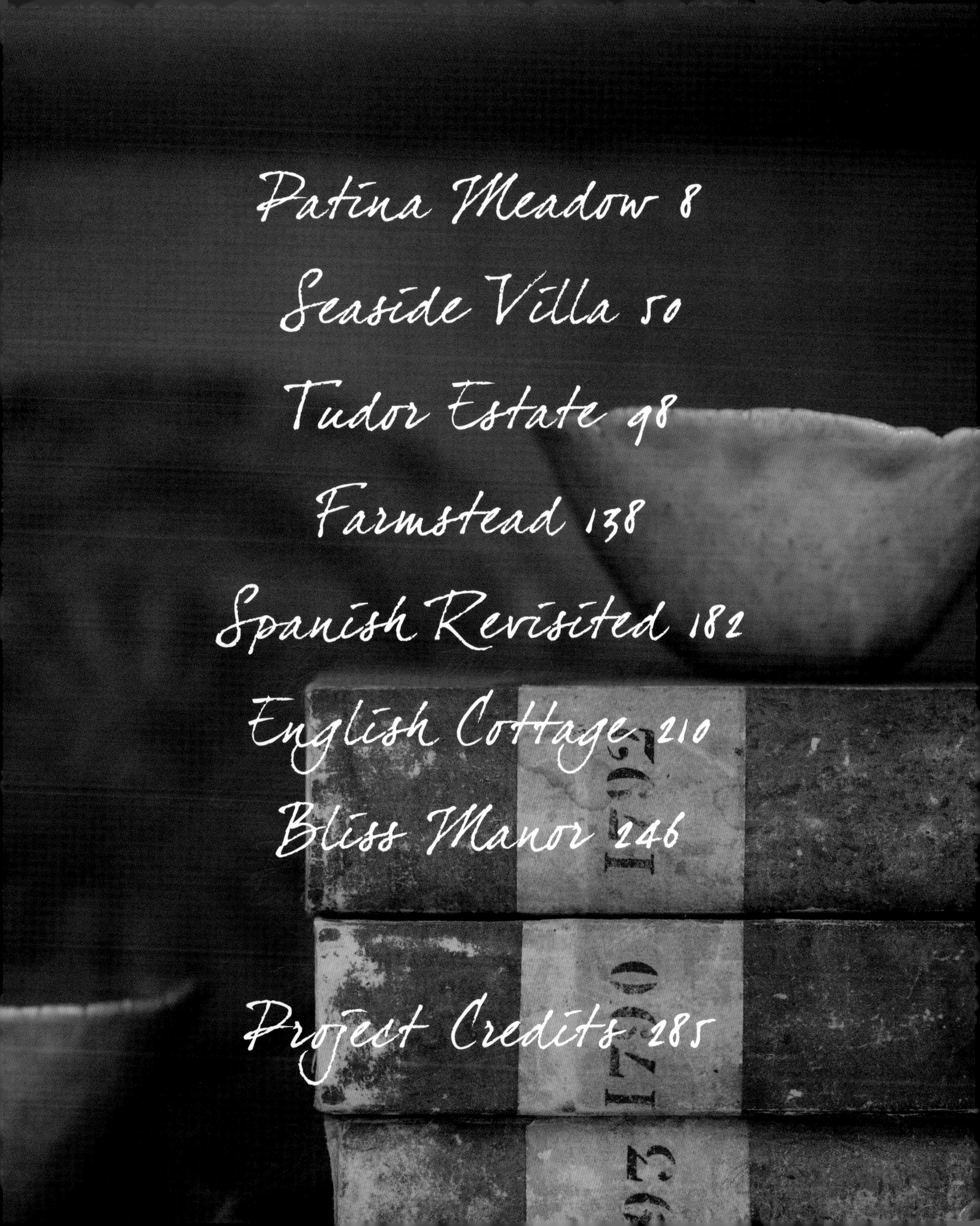

Patina Meadow 8

Seaside Villa 50

Tudor Estate 98

Farmstead 138

Spanish Revisited 182

English Cottage 210

Bliss Manor 246

Project Credits 285

Patina Meadow

3811

# Patina Meadow

Two decades ago, when I embarked on my interior design career, my architect husband Steve suggested I skip design school. Relying on my gut intuition, I had previously crafted the interiors of our homes. Steve worried a formal education might dilute this instinct, substituting it with excessive input from my head. His advice proved invaluable. Steve and I have since leaned on our heartfelt and intuitive guidance to navigate both our design and life choices. A few years ago, this was also how we knew it was time to leave Patina Farm, the property we had spent the previous ten years creating.

Many of you who follow us on social media or subscribe to my blog, *Velvet and Linen*, are familiar with the transformative decade we spent on Patina Farm. Each passing year, we became increasingly immersed in nature, dedicating more time to tending to our animals and gardens. When Leila returned home from college, she joined us at the farm and discovered her passion for gardening and pottery. Our potager became her classroom. As she delved deeper into organic farming practices, Leila and our gardens flourished like never before.

While we continued to share our life online, our growing *Velvet and Linen* community expressed a desire to visit us at the farm. We were thrilled by the demand for our small tours! Most visitors left with the same sentiment—immersing themselves in our life and the farm's beauty ignited their yearning for more nature in their lives. These tangible connections were invaluable to us all, prompting Leila, Steve, and me to envision ways to deepen them. However, faced with the rules and regulations in Ojai, we realized that our dream of hosting more visitors and offering classes at the farm wouldn't be feasible. To pursue our aspirations further, relocation became inevitable.

Through our career of assisting design clients in making life-altering decisions, coupled with our own transition from suburban life in Santa Monica to the rural haven of Ojai, we came to realize that feeling fear during times of change was a normal part of the process, and we honed our ability to navigate this path. We knew that to overcome our anxiety about leaving Patina Farm we would need to envision a compelling future that aligned with all our aspirations. Together, the three of us delved deep into the foundational principles that fill our lives with purpose. Through this introspection, we discovered four recurring themes: a profound connection to nature, a reverence for history, a desire to be of service to our community, and a shared aspiration to cultivate beauty in everyday living. Armed with these guiding principles, we embarked on designing a future that embraced these tenets and would give us the courage to move forward.

Choosing the location for our new life was easy. Over the past few years, design projects had drawn Steve and me to Leipers Fork, a magical rural community nestled in the rolling green hills south of Nashville, Tennessee. Whenever we had downtime between site visits with our clients, we'd wander into the quaint shops of this historic little town, chatting with the friendly shop owners and locals, soaking up the area's rich history. Our leisurely drives through the picturesque countryside were pure bliss, offering us the opportunity to fully appreciate the natural beauty all around us. Before we knew it, Leipers Fork felt like home, pulling us in with its welcoming embrace.

With the foundation of our guiding beliefs and the self-assurance of our intuition, we found ourselves capable of navigating decisions as they presented themselves while we prepared for our move. In our search for a new property, we discovered a charming rural homestead spanning a hundred acres in a serene valley. The landscape included several lush pastures surrounded by a majestic forest of mature trees. As visitors, we were greeted by the idyllic sight of a small bridge spanning a meandering creek that bordered the property. At the forefront stood an old red barn

and a log house dating back to the 1850s, framed by the picturesque view of pastures and woodland. Steve and I were immediately captivated, envisioning endless possibilities for this magical place. During that initial visit, we could already picture our future life unfolding on this farm, which was conveniently proximate to downtown Leipers Fork, had the potential for multiple vegetable gardens, greenhouses, and orchards, and provided spacious pastures for our animals—all within a beautiful natural setting. The decision to purchase this land felt like a natural and easy one.

Our aim for Patina Meadow was to evoke the ambiance of an authentic 1850s homestead. Retaining all original features of the vintage log cabin, we preserved the picturesque sagging roof and clad the exterior in old barn wood siding. Opening up the floor plan created a more modern sense of space while retaining the charming character of the historic structure. Our signature Patina touches, including clean white plaster walls, reclaimed wood beams, steel doors, and large-scale windows that extend nearly to the floor, were added throughout.

As with all our projects, our goal was to seamlessly connect the interior spaces with the natural world outside and offer views of the animals residing behind the house. Drawing inspiration from Patina Farm, we designed a primary bedroom and bath with a skylit shower, bathing the plaster walls in natural light. Antique furniture sourced for the sink basins added a rustic touch. In the attic above our garage, a cozy guest room was designed, inspired by our trips to the Cotswolds, featuring aged wall fabric, antique beams, and a wood stove nestled into a stone fireplace nook.

Leila, our daughter, took the lead in designing the gardens, which feature our Bloomerie greenhouses sitting on low stone walls facing our vegetable and flower garden, with willow-lined beds, all surrounded by a fence fashioned from trees found on-site. The largest structure, amusingly named the Shed, will house a pottery studio, guest rooms, and a large gathering space for future events.

As we prepared for our move, we were presented with the opportunity to consider opening a store in the center of our new hometown. What at first seemed like a crazy idea started to feel like an inevitability. Opening Patina Home and Garden would allow us to immediately become part of the Leipers Fork community and connect with locals and visitors who were also exploring a slower paced, nature-centered lifestyle. The store also offered us a space to share our view of beauty in design to a larger audience, as well as a venue in which to offer classes. During several casual discussions with the owners of the building, we learned that the future home of Patina Home and Garden had always been one of the main gathering places for the community ever since it had been the general store in the mid-1800s. The owners shared stories of its rich history, and by the end of our meetings, Steve and I began plans to create our new shop, which would allow the building to continue being a resource for visitors and locals.

In *Patina Homes & Gardens*, we offer a glimpse into our journey of navigating life transitions and assisting clients in doing the same. We delve into overcoming fears, embracing change, and crafting futures grounded in personal values. Through our experiences and insights, we hope to ignite a sense of empowerment, encouraging readers to pursue their passions and design lives aligned with their true desires.

xx
Brooke

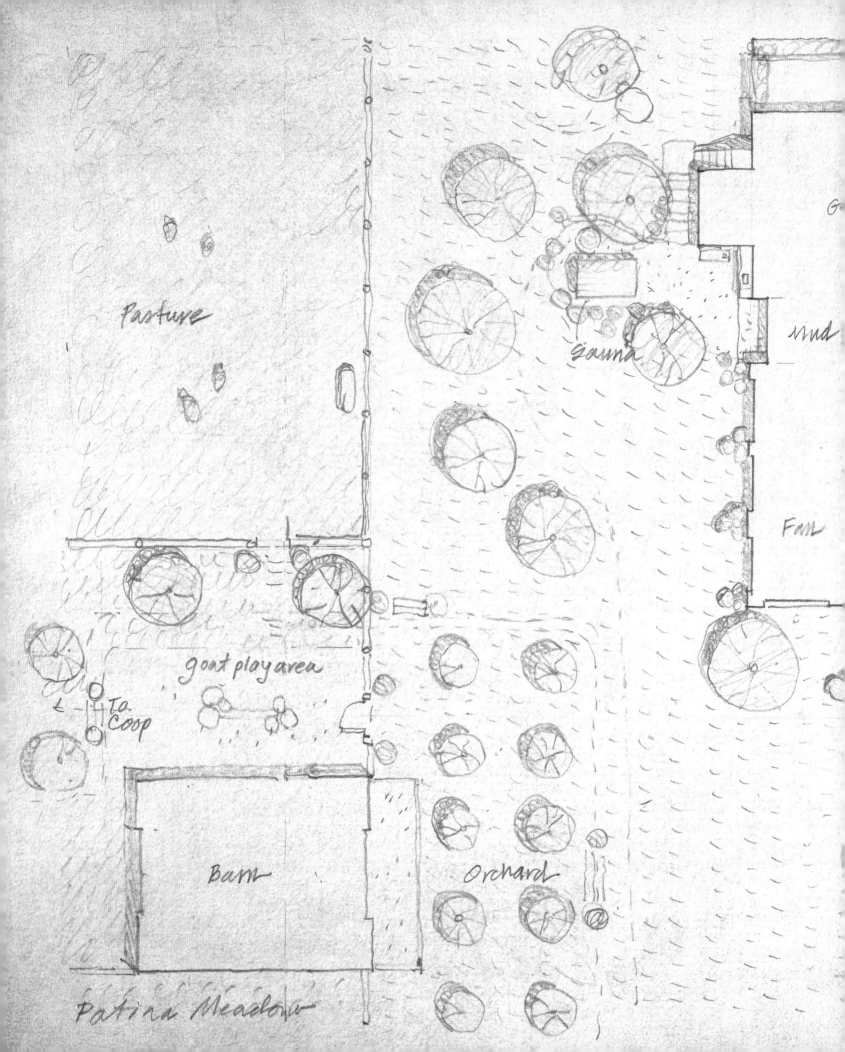

Pasture

Sauna

mud

Fan

goat play area

To Coop

Barn

Orchard

Patina Meadow

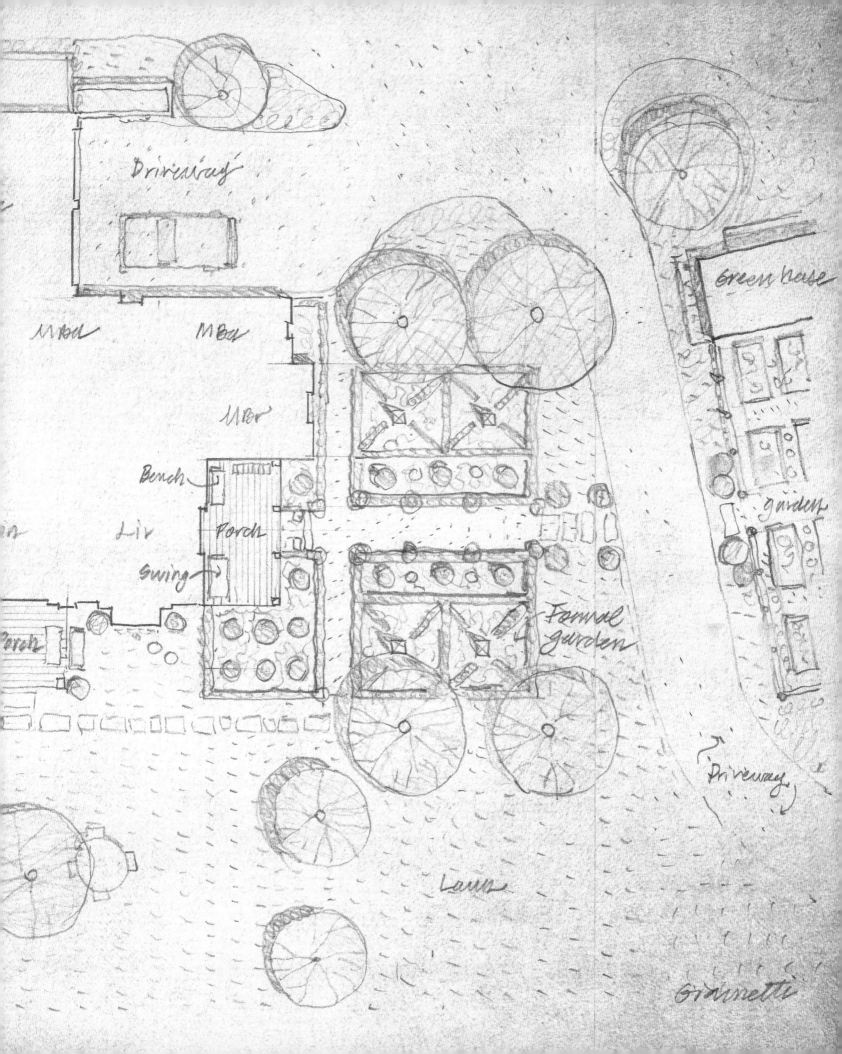

Driveway

MBa          MBa

MBr

Bench

Liv          Porch

Swing

Porch

Green house

garden

Formal garden

Driveway

Lawn

Giannetti

Seaside Villa

# Seaside Villa

On an early morning in November 2018, Steve and I received an emotional phone call from our future clients. In voices colored with loss and grief, they shared their story. Their family home was gone, instantly reduced to rubble and twisted metal by the devastating Woolsey fire that had ravaged large swaths of Los Angeles and Ventura County a few days earlier. After mourning their loss, they decided to focus their attention on what the future could hold. From the ashes, they dreamed of creating a new home. This was an opportunity to design a property that nurtured all their interests and passions. They had loved our journey of creating Patina Farm and knew that we could help them navigate the road to designing their property.

A few days after the initial call, we met the couple at their site in Malibu. The charred remains of their house juxtaposed with the magnificent views of the gentle hills and Pacific Ocean beyond was jarring. There, all together, we began the process of healing. Our clients described what they loved about this property, what made it special to them. Even during the most stressful periods of their life, a feeling of calm had washed over them as they took in the views of the water. After sharing their favorite memories, they discussed their images of their future. As they spoke, their vision began to take shape in our minds, and Steve began to sketch.

The peaceful ocean views from the property became one of the main inspirations for the design of their new home. The exterior is a mix of modern and ancient—rustic stone and smooth stucco, antique roof tiles and elegant steel windows—all in a palette that blends with the coastal landscape.

The lower ceiling height of the entry gives way to a dramatic two-story view beyond. Pale gray steel doors guide the eyes outside, down the hillside towards the water. An open floor plan ensures an unobstructed view from every vantage point. The palette of the landscape is reflected inside: varying shades of neutrals embellished with azure blues. Like the exterior, the interior is a balance of history and modernity: antique French limestone mantels and several pairs of ancient European doors balance the less-adorned architectural details such as simple iron handrails and natural oak beams.

Every space inside and outside reflects the homeowners' interests and personalities. A music studio with a New York loft vibe includes a cozy seating area surrounded by the warmth of wooden shelves filled with books and family photos; an airy art studio also works as an office. A tranquil bedroom allows them to begin and end their days appreciating the natural beauty outside, including an idyllic greenhouse for growing fresh herbs and vegetables to be used in their family's favorite recipes and an abundant rose cutting garden enhanced by rows of aromatic lavender.

As construction neared completion, it was time to add the finishing touches. Together with our clients, we layered the spaces with items we had all collected during the past couple of years—provincial pottery, textural baskets, tapestry pillows, worn leather books, faded rugs, and eclectic artwork—as well as fresh-cut flowers from the garden and greenery to connect the inside spaces with the landscape. A final shared walk all around confirmed that our design journey had come to an end. We left our clients to create the rest of their story in their new home.

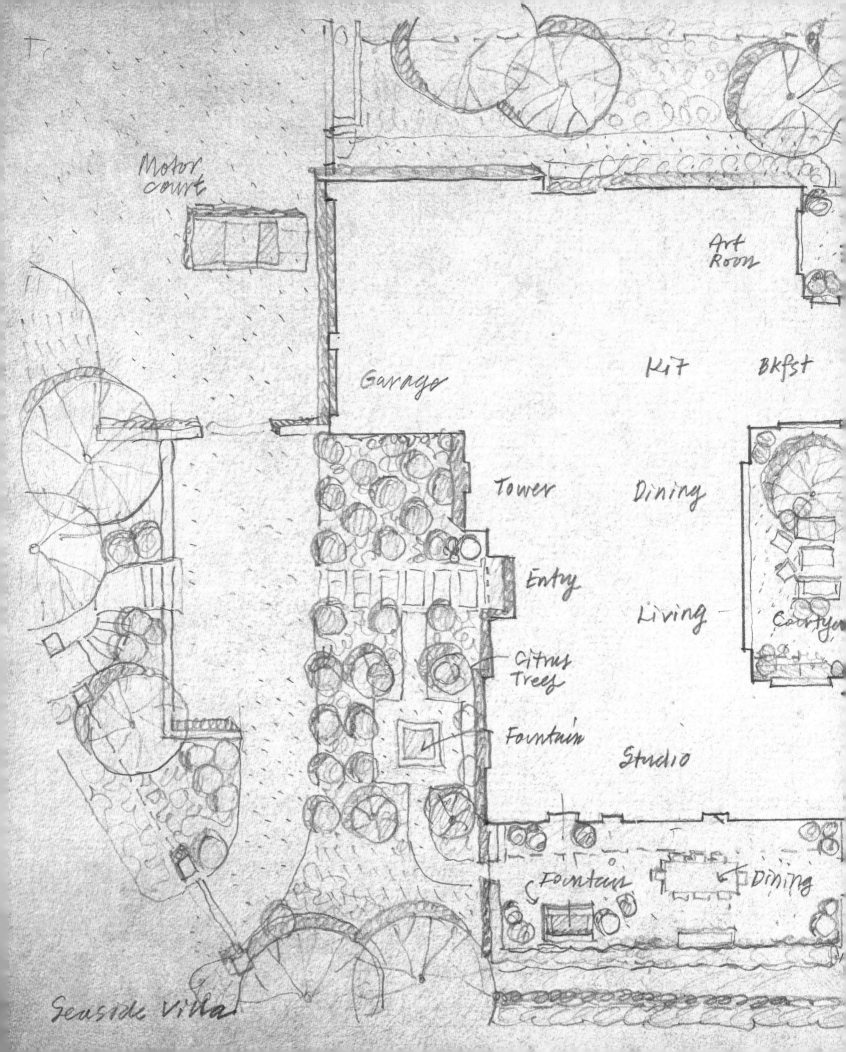

Motor
court

Art
Room

Garage

Kit

Bkfst

Tower

Dining

Entry

Living

Citrus
Trees

Courty.

Fountain

Studio

Fountain

Dining

Seaside Villa

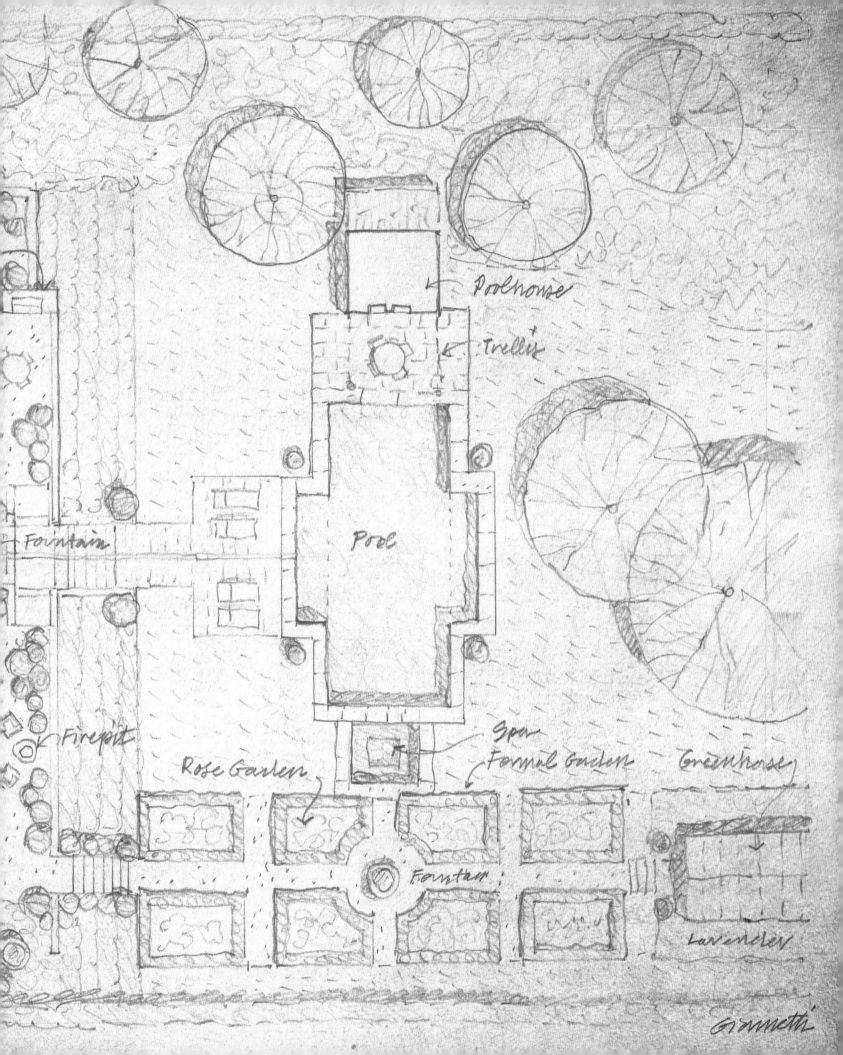

Poolhouse

Trellis

Fountain

Pool

Firepit

Rose Garden

Spa

Formal Garden

Greenhouse

Fountain

Lavender

Giannetti

Tudor Estate

# Tudor Estate

Throughout our career as designers, we have had the privilege of forming many long-term relationships with clients, which has often led to designing multiple homes for the same people as their life stories evolve. The Tudor Estate is one such project. We first crossed paths with these clients over a decade ago when they were a young married couple with a toddler son. Back then, we assisted them in transforming a modest 1920s property into their first family home, allowing them to explore their design preferences for the first time as we collaborated in selecting materials, furnishings, and artwork. Over the years, we assisted them with decorating their children's rooms and making other updates as they refined their style.

Several years had passed when the couple contacted us expressing a desire for further changes to their home. As we talked, it became evident to all of us that they had reached a point where their current home no longer met the needs of their family. It came as no surprise, then, when they subsequently called to share their plans for purchasing a new home and invited us to explore the property with them a few days later. The existing home was a 1920s English Tudor with exquisite detailing and surrounded by beautiful formal gardens. As they spoke, the overall design intent became clearer. They admired the beauty of the original architecture, but rather than attempt to replicate the traditional detailing in the interiors, they aimed to complement the original features with more modern elements.

To achieve this balance, we removed all the crown molding and baseboards. We reskimmed the interior walls with a smooth Diamond Kote finish, giving them a sculptural feel. We replaced the traditional cabinetry in the bathrooms with cleaner designs in natural white oak. We chose playful tiles from Ann Sacks to give lightness and freshness to their two sons' bathrooms, and slabs of white Calacatta marble and travertine to foster a serene spa aesthetic in the main bathroom.

The serious Tudor aesthetic was balanced through design selections with a playful attitude: curved bouclé sofas in the living room, midcentury modern–inspired shearling chairs in the guest and main bedrooms, a sculptural light fixture in the dining room, nature-inspired wallpaper on the breakfast room ceiling, and contemporary artwork throughout the home.

As we minimalized the interior architectural detailing, the material selections became the focal point in many of the rooms. In the playroom, walls of white oak, a dramatic brass fireplace surround, and a bar of vibrant stone set the entertaining tone for the space. In the pool bath, slabs of green onyx on all four walls feel enveloping. In the main powder room, iridescent tiled walls paired with an illuminated pink onyx sink welcomes visitors.

The gardens underwent a captivating transformation, evolving into a series of outdoor rooms. Approaching the front entrance, a serene path takes shelter beneath a grove of redbud trees that enhance spring with a magnificent display of purple flowers. Meandering beneath the century-old evergreens in the front yard, a stone path winds through a lush shade garden featuring elegant boxwood, fragrant jasmine, and graceful oakleaf hydrangeas. Vintage garden elements, including exquisitely aged wooden English planters and endearing stone dogs flanking the front door, instill a profound sense of history in the entrance garden. An antique faux bois bench provides an inviting resting spot, while a jovial, large-scale chicken sculpture perched on a rustic stone table adds a touch of whimsy. Rustic stone fountains strategically placed throughout the gardens contribute the delightful sound of flowing water. Large-scale boxwood topiaries lend both scale and height, and a lush wall of pale pink roses enhances the entrance to the dining room with a romantic aura.

The transformation of the Tudor Estate marries historical charm with contemporary elements, serving to illustrate that design is a dynamic force, adapting to the changing lifestyles and design sensibilities of our clients. It underscores the notion that our role as designers extends beyond aesthetics to crafting living narratives that shape homes and affect lives.

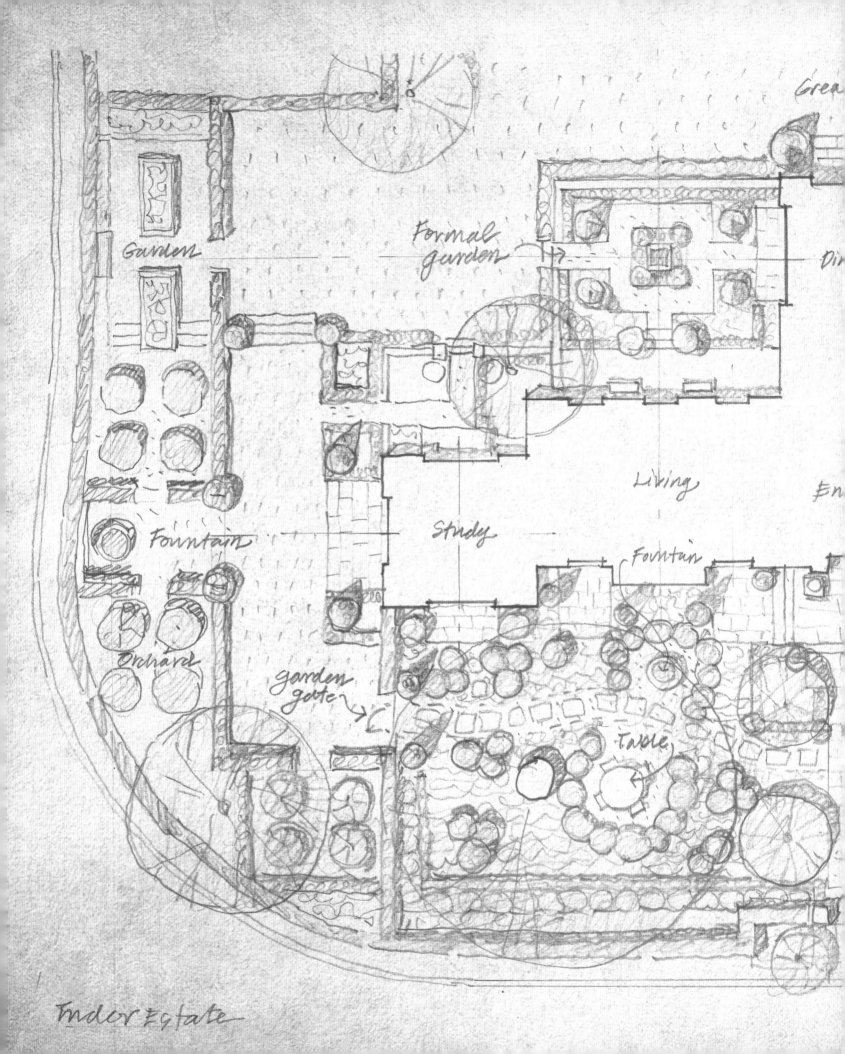

Garden

Formal garden

Grea

Din

Living

Study

En

Fountain

Fountain

Orchard

garden gate

Table

Tudor Estate

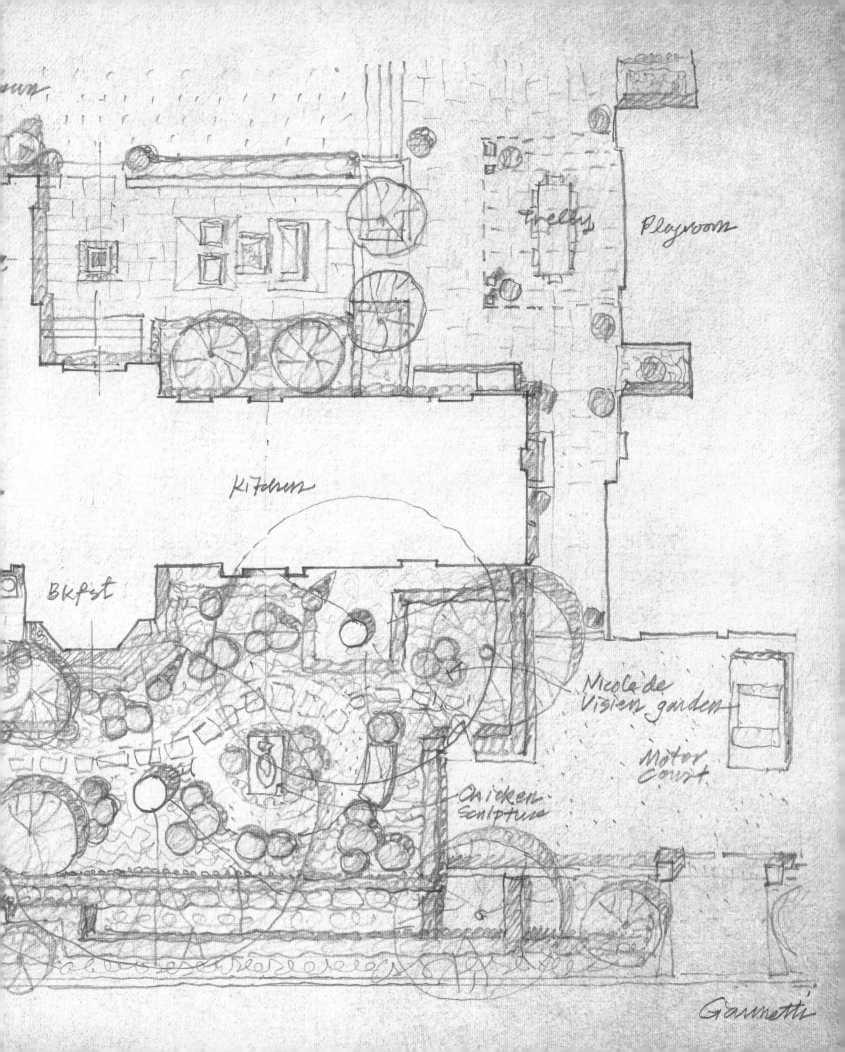

Playroom

trellis

Kitchen

Bkfst

Nicole de
Vision garden

Motor
Court

Chicken
Sculpture

Giannetti

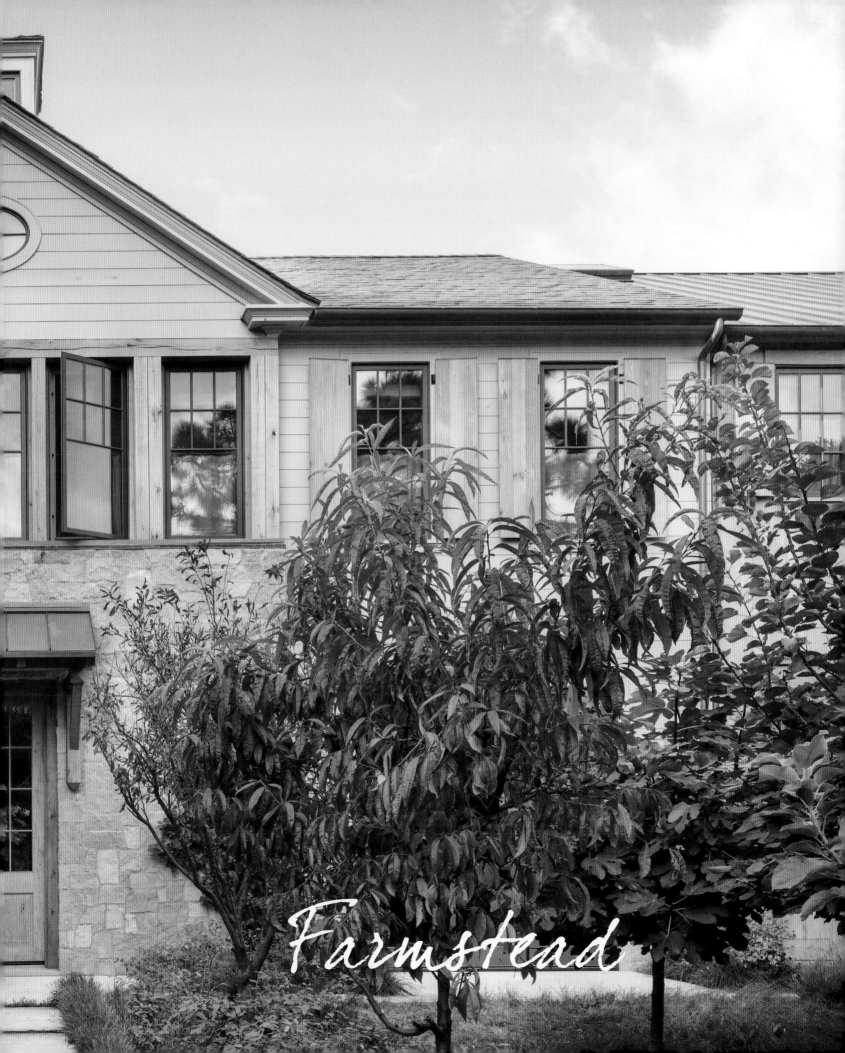

Farmstead

# Farmstead

A few years ago, a longtime client sought our help in crafting her new residence. She aspired to fashion a sanctuary for herself and her three children. Her vision for this property drew upon her West Virginian heritage and her outdoor, health-conscious lifestyle in Los Angeles, the site of her newfound abode. Her goal was to establish an exquisite estate where cherished memories, akin to those from her own upbringing, could be forged.

In alignment with her creative vision, our client's residence exhibits elements reminiscent of a rustic wood-and-stone farmhouse, seamlessly connected to an adjoining barn. Within the barn structure, the main floor serves as a garage, while the second floor boasts a spacious gym. The extensive use of natural oak and post-and-beam construction infuses the entire home with a country-inspired, relaxed aesthetic, exuding warmth and charm in every corner.

Our client's love of craftsmanship and art is manifested in the intricate details of the home. We collaborated with her talented West Virginia artisans and friends to craft custom iron fireplace screens that adorn both the living room and kitchen, drawing inspiration from the captivating trees gracing the property. Additionally, a stained-glass window holding special significance for the family was meticulously created by a local artisan friend.

Our client's vision was to maximize the integration of edible plants into the garden design. This led to the creation of an orchard featuring a diverse range of fruit trees and berry bushes lining the path to the front door. The centerpiece of the front yard is a substantial potager with ample space for cultivating vegetables and herbs to be used in the preparation of family meals. The potager structure serves a dual purpose by discreetly concealing the driveway, enhancing the overall aesthetic of the main garden entrance to the home.

The design of the back garden captures our client's passion for indoor-outdoor living. A magnificent wall of glass doors in the main living room effortlessly slides into the wall, establishing a seamless connection to the outdoor seating and dining area. Adjacent to the indoor kitchen, an outdoor kitchen is strategically placed, facilitating convenient outdoor cooking experiences. Despite the limited size of the property, the harmonious integration of indoor and outdoor spaces imparts a sense of expansiveness, both visually and through shared materiality.

To foster an intimate and welcoming atmosphere, the design unfolds into distinct, human-scale spaces. A cozy, deep azure blue library-study beckons with its comfortable L-shaped sectional and shearling chair, creating an inviting area for the family to come together. The bustling farmhouse kitchen, complete with a dedicated baking area and a wood-fired stove, seamlessly transitions into the breakfast room, which features a lounging bench and a casual dining table spacious enough for the entire family and a few visiting friends. The rich, verdant dining room walls bring the outdoors inside while providing a beautiful backdrop for our client's art collection. Upstairs, a study with a sleeping porch and a hidden reading nook nurtures the family's love of reading, adding a touch of charm to this thoughtfully designed space.

Every nook and corner of our client's home tells part of her story, capturing her history and dreams, ensuring that her home will be a cherished sanctuary for her and her children to create memories for years to come.

THE MOON IS SWIMMING
NAKED AND THE SUMMER
NIGHT IS FRAGRANT WITH
A MIGHTY EXPECTATION
OF RELIEF.
-LEONARD COHEN

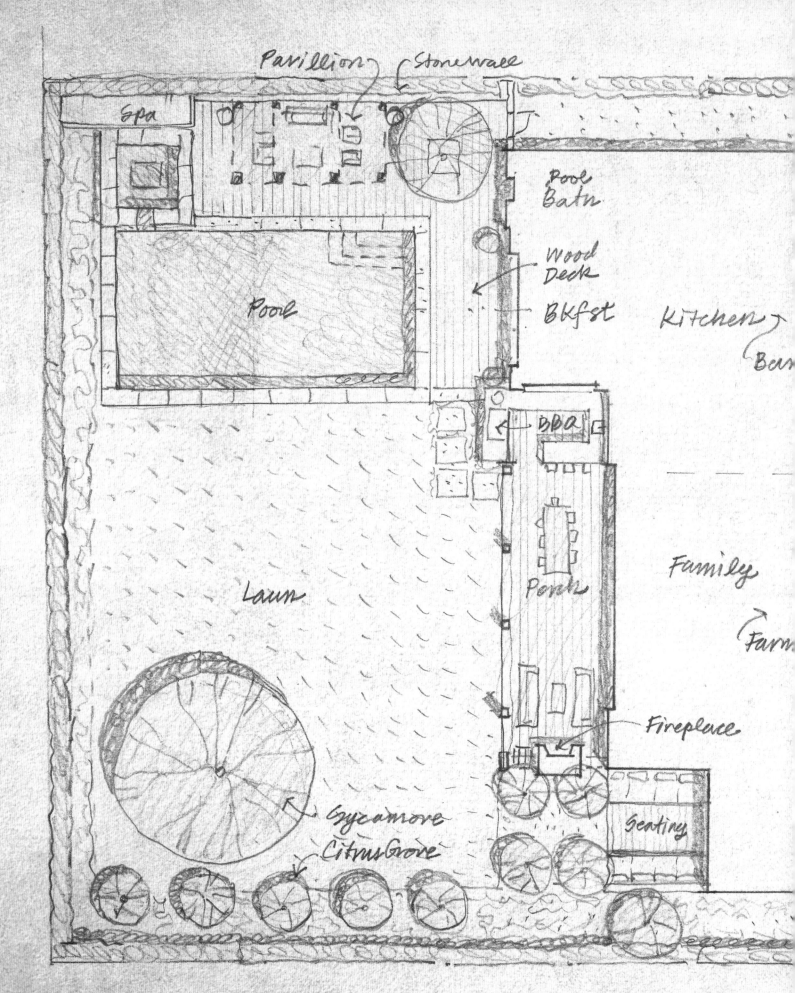

Pavillion   Stonewall

Spa

Pool Bath

Wood Deck

Bkfst

Kitchen

Bar

Pool

BBQ

Family

Farm

Porch

Lawn

Fireplace

Sycamore

Seating

Citrus Grove

Farmstead

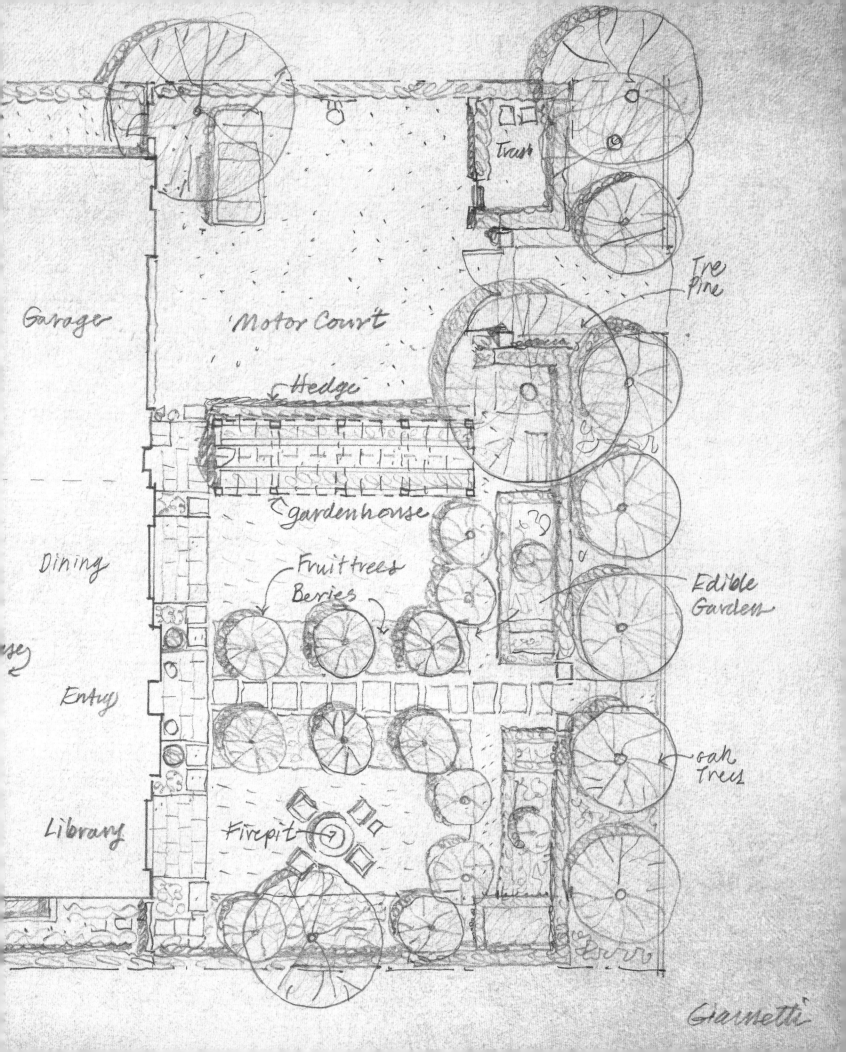

Garage

Motor Court

Trees

Tre
Pine

Hedge

gardenhouse

Dining

Fruit trees
Berries

Edible
Garden

Entry

Library

Firepit

oak
Trees

Giarnetti

Spanish Revisited

# Spanish Revisited

Steve initially designed the La Mesa project in 2006, marking the beginning of his exploration into combining traditional and modern architecture, with a goal of finding a new style that would incorporate elements of both. The original 1920s Spanish house lay in disrepair, was dark, and was disconnected from the beautiful landscape surrounding it. As it held historic significance, Steve wanted to preserve a large portion of its structure, which was, fortunately, in good condition.

The challenge was to open the house to the stunning view of the golf course and mountains beyond. Steve completely opened the back of the house, installing massive sliding glass doors that recess into the walls, connecting the indoor living spaces with the outdoor garden. Additionally, he added a full second floor to the house, carefully dismantling and reconstructing the living room ceiling using the original beams. To comply with modern earthquake codes, a massive steel frame was installed at the rear of the house, serving as both a structural necessity and a design element that imbued the house with its unique character. At the front porch, he incorporated tall arched windows made of sheets of glass that pivot in the middle, providing a subtle hint that this isn't your typical 1920s house.

Fast forward fifteen years, when the new owners reached out to Steve expressing a desire to remodel the interior and redesign the garden. Given Steve's longstanding relationship with the house, he felt compelled to ensure its preservation, and the owners were in agreement. Collaborating with the talented design team of Carrier and Company, they reimagined the interior design while retaining most of the architectural elements.

From Steve's perspective, the most significant change was the opportunity to redesign the gardens in an entirely new way. The existing front yard was originally comprised of a vast open lawn, but the new owner had a vision inspired by Patina Farm, our farm in Ojai, California—as well as images of tree-lined driveways, vegetable gardens, play areas for children, English country gardens, orchards, chicken coops, and fountains. Keeping the owners' inspiration in mind and drawing inspiration from Steve's and my recent trip to England, he devised a scheme to create a series of outdoor rooms where the elements would gradually reveal themselves as visitors explored the property.

A sycamore tree–lined driveway flanked by hedges leads to the front motor court, concealing surprises on either side. The vegetable garden, greenhouse, and children's tree house and play lawn are conveniently located near the kitchen for easy access. On the opposite side of the driveway lies the hidden English country garden, inspired by the work of Gertrude Jekyll, culminating in an unexpected rustic fountain. Adjacent to this space is a small orchard connected to a chicken coop. At the front of the house, large wooden gates open to a new courtyard featuring a grand stone fountain and patios, enhancing the indoor-outdoor connection and providing a beautiful entry.

The gardens in the backyard were simplified, creating a large lawn flowing down to the pool. Steve designed a shady outdoor dining area with fireplace and lanterns nestled under an existing mature oak tree, the perfect space to enjoy the view down the canyon to the Pacific Ocean.

Through meticulous preservation of La Mesa's historic architecture while strategically integrating contemporary features, the residence has been transformed into a space that not only respects its past but also supports the aspirations of its new owners.

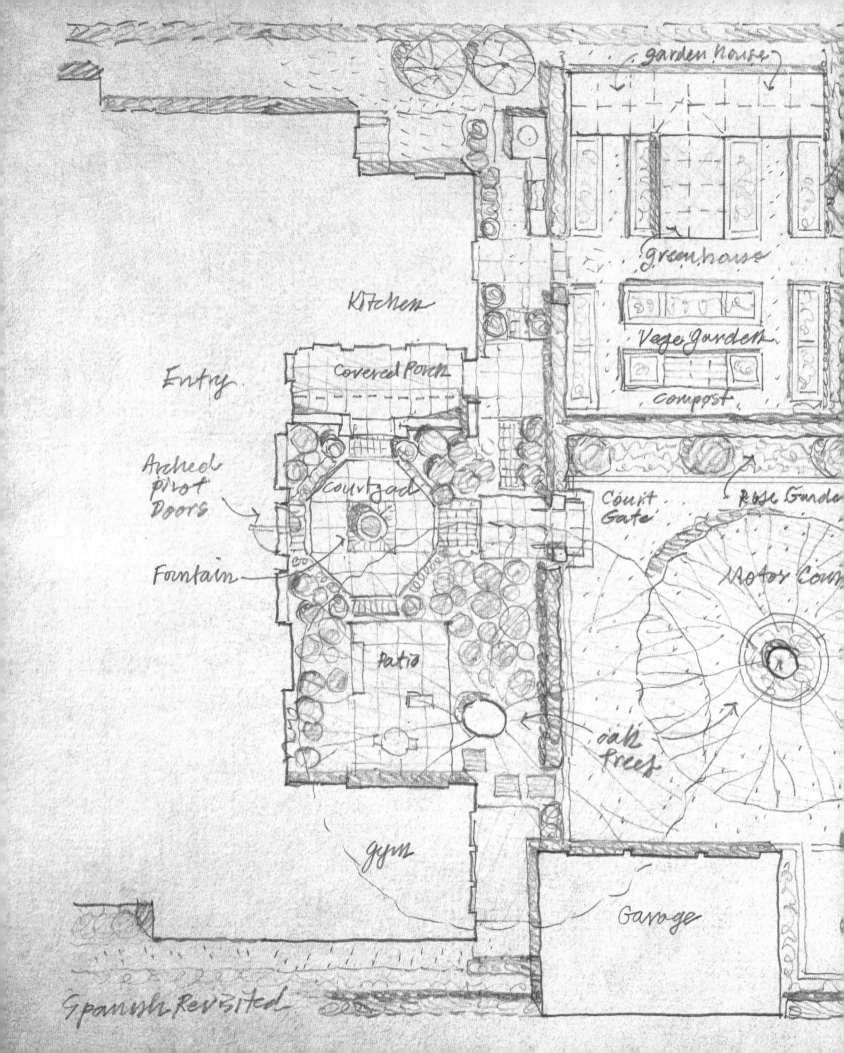

garden house

greenhouse

Vege. Garden

compost

Kitchen

Entry.

Covered Porch

Arched
Pivot
Doors

Courtyard

Fountain

Court
Gate

Rose Garden

Motor Court

Patio

oak
trees

gym

Garage

Spanish Revisited

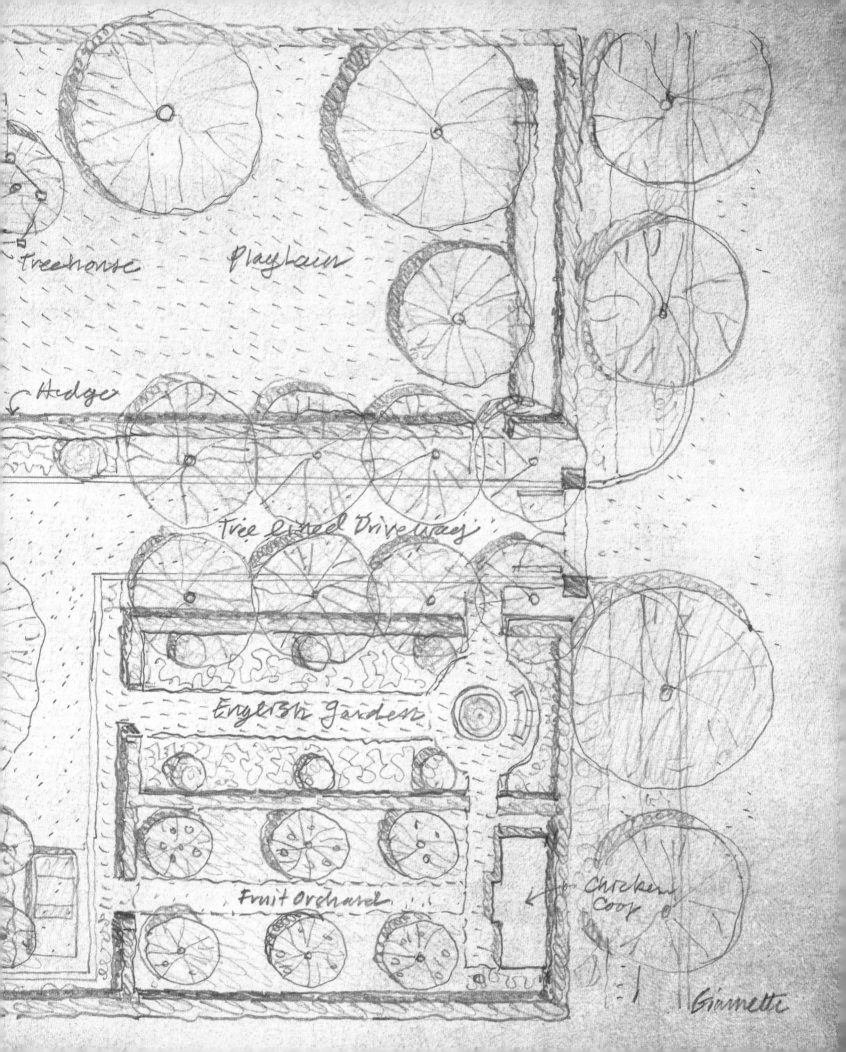

Treehouse   Playlaun

Hedge

Tree Lined Driveway

English Garden

Fruit Orchard

Chicken Coop

Giannetti

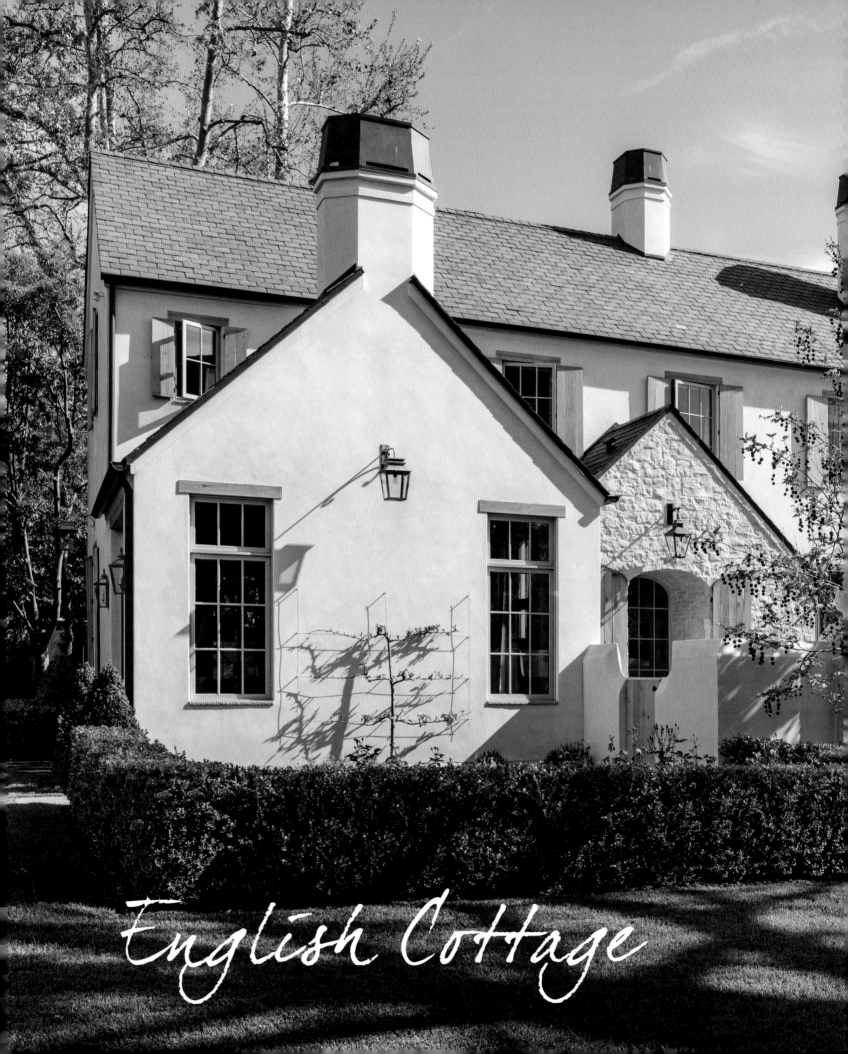

English Cottage

# English Cottage

Steve has a unique ability to visualize. Because of this gift, realtors often ask him to meet with their clients before they purchase a property to help them imagine what they could create. This is how we met our Bristol client, who was a single woman with grown children. Her existing home was charming, but it was dark and cluttered. She had a dream of living in a simpler, sparer home filled with light and being connected to gardens that felt protected from the street.

When we met her at the property, a tall hedge separated the corner lot from the street. Entering through the gate, we had a sense of privacy that was surprising for being in the middle of the city. The existing home was a teardown, but a new home could be sited to take advantage of the hedged gardens. As our client shared her vision of her new home, Steve began to sketch, giving her the confidence that this was the right site.

During our first meetings, we connected over our shared appreciation for the architecture of English country homes. Many design elements, including steeply pitched slate roofs, simple exterior massing, smaller paned windows, beamed cathedral ceilings, and unfitted kitchen cabinets, were incorporated into her new home, as well as octagonal-shaped chimneys and classic English fireplace mantel designs. Several of the interior lanterns were sourced from Jamb, one of our favorite showrooms in England, and many of our client's dark wood and bamboo antique pieces also originated from the UK. To keep the home from feeling too formal, we chose several rustic materials: wide-planked rustic oak floors, worn antique marble checkerboard stone in the entry, and a varied, undulating Zellige Moroccan tile in the powder room. The gardens also have an English aesthetic. A walled courtyard garden with clipped boxwood topiaries, illuminated with zinc wall lanterns, added to the feeling of protection from the street with an English flair.

Although our client envisioned a bright and spacious home, she also wanted cozy, intimate spaces: a separate farm kitchen connected to a comfortable breakfast room nestled by a hearth, an intimate dining space with walls of library bookshelves constructed of warm oak wood, a study for reading and movie watching with enveloping scenic wallpapered walls. All the spaces would feel cohesive, connected to each other through their limited material selections, a common color palette, and the shared views of the gardens.

A cherished portrait of our client's mother was chosen to be a focal point of the living room and the inspiration for the palette throughout the home. Pillows and lampshades made from shimmering Fortuny fabrics of silvery blues are reminiscent of her dress, and shades of warm amber like her auburn hair were incorporated in the living room. The deep blue-green used as the background of the portrait is repeated in the eighteenth-century tapestry that hangs in the dining room, as well as in the color scheme of the scenic wallpaper in the study.

To keep our client's home from feeling cluttered, we included places for her beloved collections to be appreciated—a glass kitchen hutch where her lovely hotel silver, creamware, and antique blue-and-white china can be enjoyed every day. An antique English mahogany glass cabinet, as well as the library shelves in the dining room, became homes to other cherished objects. Each piece found its place, contributing to the rich tapestry of the new home.

In the end, our collaboration with our Bristol client resulted in a home that blends the timeless charm of English country design with the comfort of modern living. Each room tells a story, reflecting her personality, memories, and cherished possessions. It's a place where warmth, elegance, and a sense of tranquility coexist, just as she had envisioned. We take pride in having helped her turn her dream into a reality, and we look forward to seeing her create new memories in this stylish sanctuary she now calls home.

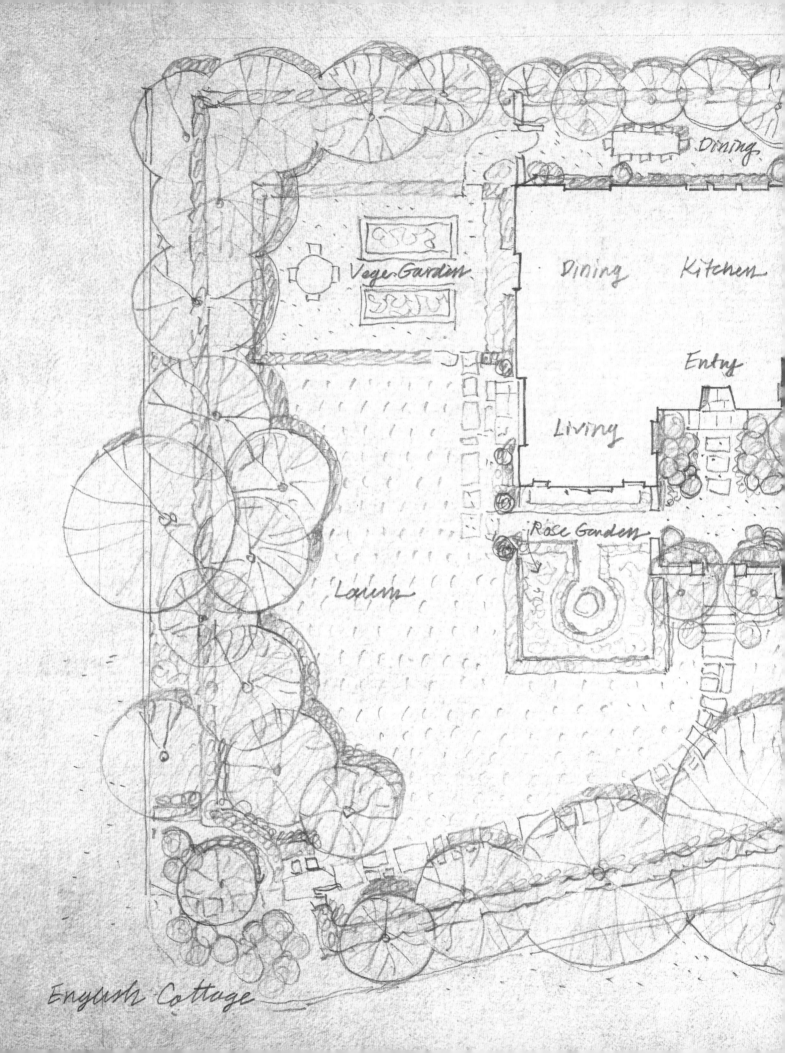

Dining

Vege Garden

Dining          Kitchen

Entry

Living

Rose Garden

Lawn

English Cottage

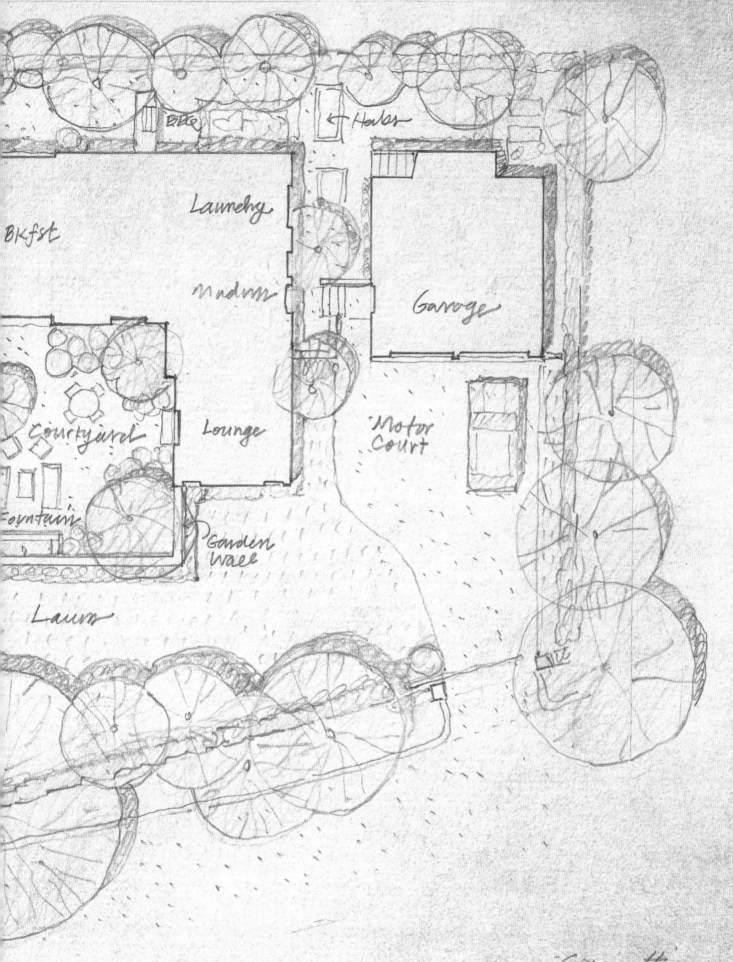

BKfst

BBQ

Heater

Laundry

Garage

Mudrm

Courtyard

Lounge

Motor
Court

Fountain

Garden
Wall

Lawn

Grinetti

Bliss Manor

# Bliss Manor

Every house comes with a unique love story, but Bliss Manor stands out as the best of them all. A few years ago, Steve received a call from the client, who excitedly shared that he had purchased a piece of land as a surprise for his wife. She had been dreaming of a new house and admired our work but hadn't gotten around to contacting us. She had even sketched a floor plan of her dream house around a courtyard and had written an extensive list of rooms that would be included in her new home. The husband sent Steve his wife's sketch and list and asked if he could design the house to surprise his wife when they visited Nashville in a few weeks. Steve accepted the fun challenge, developed some ideas, and mounted them on boards. The day before the reveal, Steve happened to meet the couple at the Antiques & Garden Show of Nashville. The wife enthusiastically pulled her floor plan from her purse and shared it with Steve, who pretended it was his first time seeing it. He complimented her on her great ideas and expressed his willingness to help someday. The next day, he set up easels at the site, and when the couple arrived and the wife saw the easels, she realized this was their new home! It was a wonderful surprise, a romantic gesture that can't be topped.

For design inspiration, Steve drew from the classic old homes of Nashville, with Cheekwood Estate & Gardens being his favorite. While his design didn't resemble Cheekwood, he aimed to infuse the DNA of a classic Southern home, emphasizing a stronger connection to the garden, a more casual indoor-outdoor flow, and a warm family atmosphere inside. He maintained classically correct proportions, detailed trim, and molding profiles while incorporating locally sourced oak to create a barn room off the main kitchen. Due to the owners having quite a large extended family and an extensive social circle, the house needed to function as both a family home and a venue for large events. A service kitchen behind the main family kitchen makes this possible, and the open layout allows large groups to gather.

We collaborated with the owners for the interior design, shopping for unique antiques from the Nashville and Atlanta markets and crafting a palette of soft, comfortable furniture to complement and enhance the classic nature of the house.

The house is nestled within a series of gardens on all sides, creating a seamless connection to the landscape. A formal dining room features a hand-painted mural of the surrounding landscape, providing an intimate dining experience. Large steel doors in the main living and dining room open onto a rear porch and courtyard with a swimming pool. A covered patio area at the back encloses the courtyard and acts as a retaining wall for the elevated landscape above.

The primary bedroom opens onto the tranquil pool courtyard, framing views of the family room beyond. A private courtyard with a fireplace off the primary bathroom allows for a wall of glass to connect to the open garden, providing a serene retreat in the mornings. The kids' wing connects to an outdoor playfield, while a study and home office have separate access and connect to a small spiral stairway leading to a below-ground wine cellar and wine room.

The second floor features a media room with an adjacent conservatory overlooking the front garden, guestrooms, an exercise room overlooking the family room, and a private spa with a view of the tower. A garden folly bunk tower at the top of the site serves as a lighthearted focal point and a destination to enjoy the view over the home and landscape beyond.

Inspired by the profound meaning of bliss—representing great joy, perfect happiness, and spiritual blessedness— our clients envisioned their home as a sanctuary where they could share countless happy moments with loved ones. Incorporating manor into the name of their home, they aimed to evoke memories of stately British homes, drawing upon the wife's childhood experiences in England. This choice reflects a sense of grace and refinement without pretension, perfectly capturing the blend of historic charm and modern luxury that characterizes the couple's dream home.

# Project Credits

## Patina Meadow

| | |
|---|---|
| ARCHITECT | Giannetti Home |
| INTERIORS | Giannetti Home |
| LANDSCAPE | Giannetti Home |
| CONTRACTOR | HHV Construction |
| PHOTOGRAPHY | Lisa Romerein |

## Seaside Villa

| | |
|---|---|
| ARCHITECT | Giannetti Home |
| INTERIORS | Giannetti Home |
| LANDSCAPE | Giannetti Home |
| CONTRACTOR | Jones Builders Group |
| PHOTOGRAPHY | Lisa Romerein |

## Spanish Revisited

| | |
|---|---|
| ARCHITECT | Giannetti Home |
| INTERIORS | Carrier and Company |
| LANDSCAPE | Giannetti Home |
| CONTRACTOR | Valle Reinis Builders |
| PHOTOGRAPHY | Lisa Romerein |

## Tudor Estate

| | |
|---|---|
| ARCHITECT | Giannetti Home |
| INTERIORS | Giannetti Home |
| LANDSCAPE | Inner Gardens |
| CONTRACTOR | Valle Reinis Builders |
| PHOTOGRAPHY | Lisa Romerein |

## English Cottage

| | |
|---|---|
| ARCHITECT | Giannetti Home |
| INTERIORS | Giannetti Home |
| LANDSCAPE | Giannetti Home |
| CONTRACTOR | Jones Builders Group |
| PHOTOGRAPHY | Lisa Romerein |

## Farmstead

| | |
|---|---|
| ARCHITECT | Giannetti Home |
| INTERIORS | Giannetti Home |
| LANDSCAPE | Giannetti Home |
| CONTRACTOR | Morrow & Morrow |
| PHOTOGRAPHY | Lisa Romerein |

## Bliss Manor

| | |
|---|---|
| ARCHITECT | Giannetti Home |
| INTERIORS | Giannetti Home |
| LANDSCAPE | Giannetti Home |
| CONTRACTOR | Jim Mullowney |
| PHOTOGRAPHY | Lisa Romerein |

It is with gratitude that we thank the following talented people for collaborating on the creation of this book:
Our dear friends Jill Cohen and Lizzy Hyland for patiently guiding us through this process for the fifth time.
Madge Baird, our fabulous editor at Gibbs Smith, for nurturing our creativity and sharing her expertise.
Lisa Romerein for beautifully capturing our clients' homes through her photography, once again.
Our talented design associates, Ryan Oliva, Laura Putnam, Andrew Mitchell, Blenda Mitchell, Renata Costa, Nick Giannetti, Danielle Baker, and Rhett Putnam for helping us turn our clients' dreams into reality.

One of the highlights of relocating to Tennessee has been the opening of our shop, Patina Home & Garden, in the charming historic town of Leipers Fork. This store truly reflects our life philosophy and allows us to engage with our community while sharing the blooms and organically cultivated produce grown by Leila at our farm, Patina Meadow. It serves as a creative space for Brooke and Steve to craft distinctive Patina style vignettes using carefully selected items.

If you're ever in Tennessee, we invite you to visit us at Patina Home & Garden! Meeting so many of you has been a privilege, and we cherish the stories you share.

For more insights into our store and to keep up with the latest events, visit our website at PatinaHomeandGarden.com or follow us on Instagram at @patinahomeandgarden. We love to stay connected with our community!

xx,
Brooke (@velvetandlinen)
Steve (@stevegiannetti)
Leila (@leilarosegiannetti)

First Edition
28 27 26 25 24      5 4 3 2 1

Text © 2024 Brooke Giannetti and Steve Giannetti
Illustrations © 2024 Steve Giannetti
Photographs © 2024 Lisa Romerein

Published by
Gibbs Smith
570 North Sportsplex Dr.
Kaysville, Utah 84037
1.800.835.4993 orders
www.gibbs-smith.com

Developed in collaboration with Jill Cohen Associates, LLC
Design by Steve Giannetti

Library of Congress Control Number: 2024937046
ISBN: 978-1-4236-6793-3

Printed and bound in China
Printed on FSC®-certified and other controlled material

Bliss Manor

Giannetti

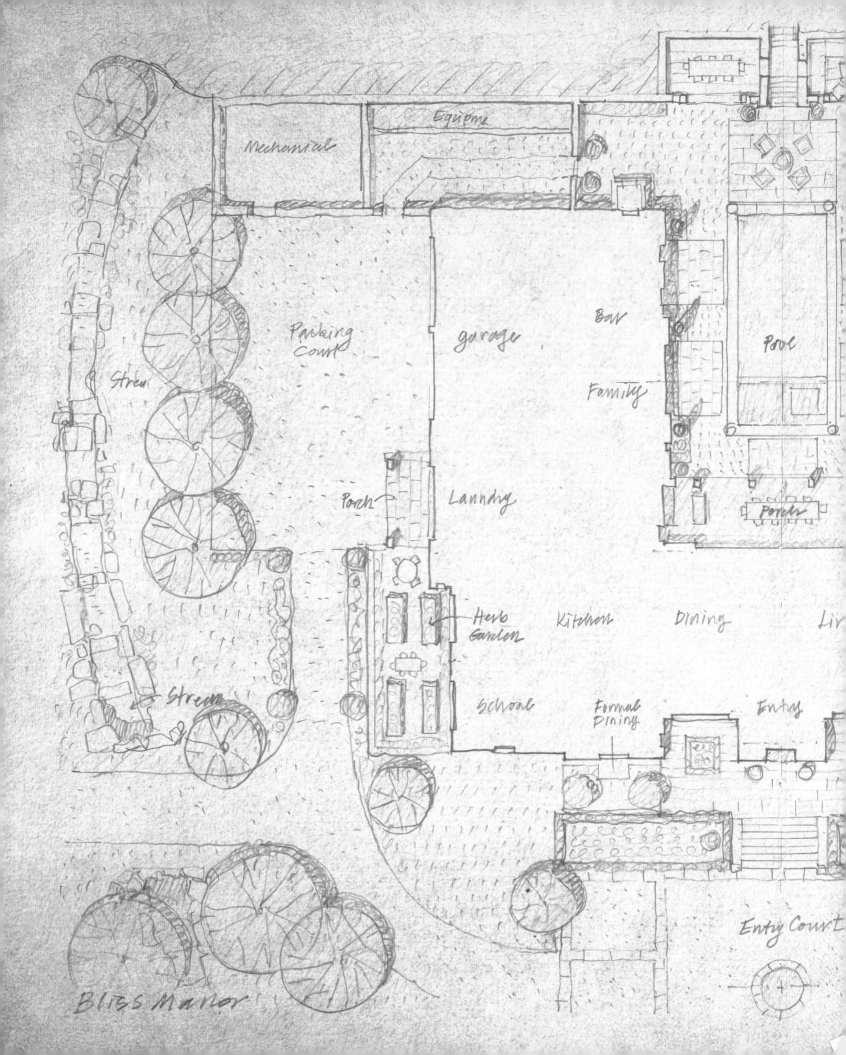

Mechanical

Equeme

Parking
Court

Stream

Bar

garage

Pool

Family

Porch

Laundry

Porch

Herb
Garden

Kitchen

Dining

Liv

Stream

School

Formal
Dining

Entry

Bliss Manor

Entry Court